COUNTRIES OF THE WORLD

Costa Rica

Gareth Stevens Publishing
A WORLD ALMANAC EDUCATION GROUP COMPANY

About the Author: Nicole Frank is a graduate of Northwestern University. She has visited many countries and studied several languages. She now divides her time between writing and traveling.

Acknowledgments: The publishers are indebted to www.costarica.com for input on Costa Rica.

PICTURE CREDITS

A.N.A Press Agency: 26, 27, 60, 61, 72
Archive Photos: 5 (bottom), 16, 17, 35, 38, 74, 75, 76 (bottom), 77, 78, 82, 83
Camera Press: 15 (bottom)
CanaPress Photo Service: 53, 71, 80, 81
DDB Stock Photo: 15 (top), 44, 45
Focus Team–Italy: 1, 3 (center), 5 (top), 19 (bottom), 23, 29, 37, 46, 54, 55 (both), 67, 73
Robert Francis: 19 (top)
Dave G. Houser: cover, 2, 7, 30, 34, 40, 43, 52, 62, 69, 84
The Hutchison Library: 20, 33, 47, 66, 87, 91
Björn Klingwall: 21, 28
Jason Laure: 39, 85
NASA: 50, 51
Michael J. Pettypool: 9
Pietro Scozzari: 42, 48, 49, 63
David Simson: 22, 24, 25
Alejandro Solorzano: 90
South American Pictures: 13, 14, 31, 59
The Tico Times: 70
Topham Picturepoint: 3 (top and bottom), 10, 11, 18, 56, 57, 58, 64, 68, 76 (top), 79
Trip Photographic Library: 6, 89
Vision Photo Agency/Hulton Getty: 12, 65
Nik Wheeler: 4, 8, 32, 36, 41

Digital Scanning by Superskill Graphics Pte Ltd

Written by
NICOLE FRANK

Edited by
LEELA VENGADASALAM

Designed by
JAILANI BASARI

Picture research by
SUSAN JANE MANUEL

First published in North America in 2000 by
Gareth Stevens Publishing
A World Almanac Education Group Company
1555 North RiverCenter Drive, Suite 201
Milwaukee, Wisconsin 53212 USA

For a free color catalog describing
Gareth Stevens' list of high-quality books
and multimedia programs, call
1-800-542-2595 (USA) or
1-800-461-9120 (CANADA).
Gareth Stevens Publishing's
Fax: (414) 225-0377.

© **TIMES MEDIA PRIVATE LIMITED 2000**
Originated and designed by
Times Editions
An imprint of Times Media Private Limited
A member of the Times Publishing Group
Times Centre, 1 New Industrial Road
Singapore 536196
http://www.timesone.com.sg/te

Library of Congress Cataloging-in-Publication Data
Frank, Nicole.
Costa Rica / by Nicole Frank.
p. cm. -- (Countries of the world)
Includes bibliographical references and index.
Summary: An introduction to the geography, history, government, lifestyles, culture, and current issues of Costa Rica.
ISBN 0-8368-2323-0 (lib. bdg.)
1. Costa Rica--Juvenile literature. [1. Costa Rica.] I. Title.
II. Countries of the world (Milwaukee, Wis.)
F1543.2.F73   2000
927.86--dc21   00-026578

Printed in Malaysia

1 2 3 4 5 6 7 8 9 04 03 02 01 00

Contents

AN OVERVIEW OF COSTA RICA

Costa Rica is a small country in Central America, renowned for its rain forests and animal life. Some travelers to the country call it Earth's national park. The name Costa Rica, which means "rich coast," dates back to the sixteenth century, when Christopher Columbus and other adventurers believed the region contained an abundance of gold. Although the explorers never found the gold they sought, the name stuck.

Costa Rica's indigenous peoples number less than 3 percent of the population and live mainly in remote areas. *Mestizos* (mays-TEE-sohs), or people of Spanish and Indian parentage, make up more than 90 percent of the population. Their diverse history and traditions make Costa Rica a truly vibrant country.

Opposite: The sandy beaches and clear waters of the Nicoya Peninsula attract both tourists and locals.

Below: Costa Ricans are peace-loving people. They strive to avoid confrontation, and the country has no military.

THE FLAG OF COSTA RICA

Like the flags of Guatemala, Honduras, Nicaragua, and El Salvador, the Costa Rican flag is based on the blue and white flag of the United Provinces of Central America, also known as the Central American Federation. All five countries were members of the federation, from its start in 1823 until it was dissolved in 1840. The blue stands for faith and justice, while the white represents purity and fairness. The red band, a tribute to the 1848 revolution in Europe, was added when the new flag was adopted that same year. The flag also contains the state's national shield in a white disk.

Geography

Beaches and Mountains

With a land area of 19,730 square miles (51,101 square kilometers), Costa Rica is one of the smallest countries in Central America. It is bordered by Nicaragua on the north, the Caribbean Sea along its eastern coastline, Panama to the south, and the Pacific Ocean along its western coastline. From some vantage points in Costa Rica, it is possible to see the beautiful beaches of both the Pacific and Caribbean coasts at the same time.

Costa Rica has two major mountain ranges: the Cordillera Volcánica and the Cordillera de Talamanca. The Cordillera Volcánica consists of three continuous ranges: the Cordillera de Guanacaste, the Cordillera de Tilarán, and the Cordillera Central. These ranges contain seven active volcanoes, of which Arenal Volcano, in the Cordillera de Guanacaste, is the most volatile. Cerro Chirripó, in the Cordillera de Talamanca, is the highest peak in Costa Rica at 12,530 feet (3,819 meters).

VOLCANOES

Costa Rica has seven active volcanoes that spit out clouds of gas and sediment from time to time. Despite warning signs at the feet of the volcanoes, visitors can pay a fee to go up to the craters.
(A Closer Look, page 72)

Below: **Tortuga Island, located off the southern Nicoya coast, is a private nature reserve operated by a San José family.**

The Regions

Costa Rica has three geographical regions: the Pacific coast, the central highlands, and the Caribbean lowlands. The Pacific coast has steep cliffs, sandy beaches, and three peninsulas, one of which Costa Rica shares with Panama. The other two peninsulas are the Nicoya Peninsula and the Osa Peninsula. Off the southwestern coast of the Nicoya Peninsula is the Isla del Coco, or Cocos Island. This island, which became part of Costa Rica in 1900, is the largest uninhabited island in the world.

In the central highlands of Costa Rica is the Meseta Central, a series of valleys bordered by the Cordillera Central and the Cordillera de Talamanca. San José, Costa Rica's capital, as well as the cities of Cartago, Heredia, and Alajuela, are all found here. For centuries, volcanic ash has enriched the soil of the Meseta Central, making it a prime area for growing coffee and sugarcane. Today, Meseta Central is home to more than two-thirds of Costa Rica's population.

The Caribbean lowlands along the eastern coast consist of flat plains irrigated by streams from the central highlands. Lowland areas in the northeast do have a few hills and volcanoes.

Above: **Poás Volcano, located north of the city of Alajuela, is 8,885 feet (2,708 m) high. It has one of the world's largest volcanic craters. The green lake in the crater is visible on a clear day.**

COCOS ISLAND

Cocos Island, the largest uninhabited island in the world, lies in the Pacific Ocean and belongs to Costa Rica. The island, now a national park, is covered with tropical vegetation and magnificent waterfalls. Despite rumors of hidden pirate treasures on the island, no one has yet been successful in finding them.

(A Closer Look, page 53)

Climate

Costa Rica is just eight degrees north of the equator, so the climate is tropical all year round but varies according to rainfall and elevation.

Seasons are defined by the amount of rainfall the country receives in each particular period. *Verano* (vay-RAH-noh), or summer, refers to the dry period between December and May, while *invierno* (een-vee-AIR-noh), or "winter," is the wet, rainy season between June and November. Costa Rica tends to receive the most rainfall in September and October, when it often rains continuously for days.

The Coasts and Highlands

The Caribbean coast receives the most rain. The average temperature along the coast is about 84° Fahrenheit (29° Celsius), while the average temperature in the highlands is 72° F (22° C). Elevation determines the temperature of a region. The higher the land, the lower the temperatures.

Above: Trees bloom all year round in Costa Rica's warm weather.

THE QUETZAL

Believed to be the most magnificent bird in the Western Hemisphere, the pigeon-sized quetzal is one of Costa Rica's national treasures. Costa Rica has ten of the forty species of quetzal found worldwide.
(A Closer Look, page 64)

Plants and Animals

Costa Rica is famous for its lush rain forests. They once covered much of the country, but, by the early 1980s, rain forests accounted for less than 20 percent of the country's land area. Although the law protects the remaining rain forests from any type of destruction, deforestation continues to be a big problem for Costa Rica.

An incredible 2,000 species of trees grow throughout Costa Rica. This habitat supports about 10,000 types of plants and about 1,200 varieties of orchids. Many of the plants have medicinal value, making them an important resource for the country's health care industry.

Animals, such as howler monkeys, jaguars, sloths, anteaters, manatees, and turtles, are also found in the wild expanses of Costa Rica. The country has 162 species of snakes, of which twenty-two are poisonous. The poison dart frog, a small animal with bright blue or red skin, also lives in Costa Rica.

SEA TURTLES

Sea turtles are on the world's endangered list of animals, although programs to conserve them are well underway. Costa Rica is home to five species of turtles. These turtles nest on the Caribbean and Pacific coasts.
(A Closer Look, page 68)

Below: **An animal unique to Costa Rica is the three-toed sloth.**

History

When the Spaniards landed in Costa Rica in the sixteenth century, more than 27,000 Indians lived there. The Indians turned out beautiful metalwork and ceramics. They were roughly divided into five groups: the Chorotega, Carib, Boruca, Corobicí, and Nahua. These groups often fought against each other for control of territories.

Spanish Invasion

On September 18, 1502, Christopher Columbus, on his fourth voyage for the Spanish Crown, landed in what is now the port city of Limón. The Indians greeted him with gifts of gold. Thinking the land was full of riches, Columbus named it "Rich Coast of Veragua." The larger area — present-day Costa Rica, Panama, and other unexplored parts of the isthmus — was called Veragua. Costa Rica later turned out to be one of Spain's poorest overseas colonies.

Left: **Christopher Columbus was the first European to set foot on the coast of Costa Rica.**

The Spaniards found it difficult to bring the indigenous peoples under their control. The local peoples, despite frequent infighting, joined forces to resist Spanish domination. In 1539, the area that is now Costa Rica was separated from Veragua and was officially named Costa Rica. It was not until 1561, however, that Governor Juan de Cavallón succeeded in colonizing the Caribbean coast of Costa Rica. He established the settlement of Garcimuñoz but left the following year. In 1562, Juan Vasquez de Coronado replaced de Cavallón as governor of Costa Rica and, in 1564, relocated Garcimuñoz to the Meseta Central. The settlement, renamed Cartago, provided an agricultural base from which the Spaniards could further colonize Costa Rica.

In this period, large numbers of Indians died due to disease, tribal warfare, and battling the Spaniards. The remaining Indians, especially the Chorotegas, became Christians. As Christians, they were allowed to remain in their villages or move into the Hispanic settlements, where they quickly assimilated through intermarriage and formed the mestizo peoples.

Above: **Christopher Columbus never found the gold he sought in Costa Rica.**

Declaring Independence

In 1821, with the Spanish Empire weakened by Napoleon Bonaparte's invasion of Spain, Mexico and the Central American provinces declared independence. Costa Rica immediately joined the Mexican Empire, despite a dispute among its four major cities. Heredia and Cartago wanted to be part of the Empire. Alajuela and San José did not. In 1822, a civil war broke out between the cities. Alajuela and San José won the war. In March 1823, Costa Rica left the Mexican Empire and joined four other Central American countries to form the United Provinces of Central America. It broke away from this union in 1838 to become an independent country.

The Coffee Elite

In the 1840s, San José became the center of coffee production in Costa Rica, and Costa Rica began exporting coffee to the newly created coffee market in England. José María Castro Madriz, who became the first president of Costa Rica in 1847, promoted coffee planting in the country. In 1849, his successor, Juan Rafael Mora Porras, followed his lead, and, by the mid-1800s, a small group of coffee barons had emerged.

In 1855, a Nicaraguan rebel faction hired William Walker, an American, to overthrow Nicaragua's president. After defeating his opponent, Walker named himself president and took control of Nicaragua. In 1856, Walker attempted to invade Costa Rica's province of Guanacaste. Costa Rican forces, led by Juan Rafael Mora Porras, struck back fiercely. One of the defenders, Juan Santamaría, set fire to Walker's stronghold in the town of Rivas across the Nicaraguan border. Walker and his troops were defeated, and Santamaría became a national hero in Costa Rica.

Although he won the battle, the high price of the victory, in terms of the soldiers who died in the war, led to Mora Porras's fall from power. In 1870, the presidency was seized by General Tomás Guardia Gitiérrez, who held the reins of power until 1882.

Left: **In 1856, William Walker proclaimed himself ruler of Nicaragua and tried to invade Guanacaste in Costa Rica.**

Left: **This statue commemorates Juan Rafael Mora Porras, who led Costa Ricans to victory in the battle against William Walker.**

Guardia's greatest contribution to Costa Rica was a railway project he initiated in 1872. The Atlantic Railway, which extended from the Meseta Central to the Caribbean coast, took eighteen years to complete.

In 1889, a new, liberal constitution was written. Costa Rica continued to grow, with large numbers of European immigrants settling in the country. The following year, the first free elections in Central American history were held. Costa Rica became the region's only true democracy.

In the late 1920s, Costa Rica began to experience economic difficulties. The worldwide economic crisis of 1929 brought about a fall in coffee prices. Lower profits and fewer exports hurt the Costa Rican economy. In 1940, Rafael Angel Calderón Guardia became president. He amended the constitution and helped establish a system of social security.

THE ATLANTIC RAILWAY

The Atlantic Railway took eighteen years to construct and cost the lives of some 4,000 people. The railway was built to transport goods from San José to the city of Limón.

(A Closer Look, page 44)

Calderón ran for president again in 1948 but was defeated
by rival Otilio Ulate Blanco. Calderón refused to accept the
defeat, and a civil war ensued. José Figueres Ferrer, a landowner,
gathered a group of 600 men, mostly students, to form the
National Liberation Party (PLN) to defend Ulate's government.
After forty-four days of fighting, the war ended. Figueres took
power after what is believed to be the bloodiest period in Costa
Rica's history.

In 1955, supporters of Calderón invaded Costa Rica from
across the Nicaraguan border and captured the town of Quesada.
Figueres sought the assistance of the United States, and, in 1956,
the leaders of Nicaragua and Costa Rica signed a treaty of
friendship. Figueres was voted out of office in 1958, but when the
succeeding president could not lower Costa Rica's national debt,
the PLN regained power in the 1962 election. A decade of peace
and prosperity followed.

The 1980s and 1990s were characterized by political conflicts
in the Central American region, such as civil wars in Nicaragua
and El Salvador. Costa Rica, however, enjoyed peace and
prosperity. In 1986, PLN candidate Oscar Arias Sánchez became
president of Costa Rica. He revived the economy and was a
mediator in Nicaragua's and El Salvador's civil wars. For his
efforts, he was awarded the 1987 Nobel Prize for Peace. José
María Figueres Olsen, son of José Figueres, won the presidency
in 1994 and continued his term in office until early 1998. Miguel
Angel Rodriguez is the current president of Costa Rica.

JOSÉ FIGUERES

**Known as the grandfather
of democracy in Costa
Rica, José Figueres was
president of Costa Rica
from 1948 to 1949, 1953
to 1958, and 1970 to 1974.
He made many social and
economic reforms during
his terms in office.**

(A Closer Look, page 56)

Juan Santamaría (c. 1839–1856)

Juan Santamaría rose to fame during the war against William Walker, an American who, in 1856, proclaimed himself ruler of Nicaragua. Juan Santamaría carried a torch in the battle at Rivas, in Nicaragua, and set fire to enemy buildings. His bravery led to the defeat of Walker and his troops. Santamaría died during the battle but became Costa Rica's first national hero — a symbol of patriotism and bravery. The San José International Airport is named after Santamaría. A museum and a statue of Santamaría can be found in his home town, Alajuela. The town celebrates El Día de Juan Santamaría, or the Day of Juan Santamaría, every year in April.

Juan Santamaría

Sonia Picado Sotela (1936–)

Sonia Picado Sotela has held several powerful political positions in Costa Rica and has been a champion of human rights around the world. In 1980, she became the first woman dean of a law school in Central America. She has also served as executive director for the Inter-American Institute of Human Rights and vice president for the Inter-American Court of Human Rights. In 1993, Picado Sotela won the United Nations (UN) Human Rights Prize. In 1996, she became Costa Rica's ambassador to the United States. She is currently a member of the Costa Rican Congress.

Oscar Arias Sánchez (1940–)

Oscar Arias Sánchez was born into a wealthy Costa Rican family. He studied law and economics at Boston University and, after receiving his doctorate from the University of Essex, London, entered politics. Arias Sánchez worked for the PLN, and, in 1972, he became a minister on the Council of Government. In the next decade, he held many political positions. In 1986, Arias Sánchez was elected president of Costa Rica and was instrumental in the Central American peace process. In 1987, he won the Nobel Prize for Peace. With the prize money, he set up a foundation for peace and progress. Since his term in office, Arias Sánchez has continued with his peace work, concentrating on demilitarizing Haiti and Panama and establishing a code of conduct on arms transfers.

Oscar Arias Sánchez

Government and the Economy

Three Branches of Government

Costa Rica is a democratic republic. The country has maintained peace for fifty years, despite conflicts in the neighboring countries of Panama and Nicaragua. Its constitution, which was adopted in 1949, established independent executive, legislative, and judicial branches of government.

The executive branch is made up of the president, two vice presidents, and the *Consejo de Gobierno* (kohn-SAY-ho day goh-bee-AIR-noh), or the Council of Government. This council consists of eighteen ministers who enforce national laws and set the country's foreign policies. The council also has the power to veto bills passed by the legislature. The president is elected directly by the people to a four-year term. To qualify for office, the presidential candidate must receive at least 40 percent of the vote. If no single candidate can secure this percentage, a second election is held to decide between the top two candidates.

Left: **Costa Rica has maintained a democracy and conducted free and fair elections for the past fifty years. Presidential elections are held every four years in February.**

The legislative branch has a single body of lawmakers called the Legislative Assembly. The assembly has fifty-seven members, who have the power, with a two-thirds majority vote, to override presidential vetos. The legislative branch has numerous other duties and powers, including the power to impeach the president.

The Supreme Court leads the country's judicial system and is divided into three chambers. The first chamber handles appeals against administrative and civil judgments made by the lower courts, the second handles appeals on family matters, and the third handles criminal appeals.

Costa Rica has two major political parties: the PLN and the Social Christian Unity Party (PUSC). Although there are nine other political parties in the country, the PLN and PUSC receive the majority of votes. These two parties also control the majority of seats in the Legislative Assembly.

Although Costa Rica does not have a military, the country maintains a large police force, and the constitution says that emergency forces may be organized for national defense.

Above: **On February 1, 1998, Miguel Angel Rodriguez of the PUSC thanked supporters after a preliminary count gave him 47.4 percent of the vote in Costa Rica's presidential election. The PUSC eventually won the election.**

Economy

Costa Rica's economy depends primarily on tourism, agriculture, and cattle. In the 1950s, to expand its export market in beef, large areas of land were cleared for raising cattle. Clearing the land, however, led to problems of soil erosion and deforestation. Also, because the cattle industry did not employ large numbers of workers, only the wealthy landowners benefited. Today, beef is Costa Rica's third largest export, after bananas and coffee.

Exports and Imports

The banana industry, dominated by Chiquita Brands, Del Monte Foods, and Standard Fruit/Dole, made U.S. $580 million in 1995 and accounted for one-fifth of Costa Rica's exports. Besides traditional exports, such as bananas, coffee, and beef, non-traditional exports, such as plastics, pineapples, and electronics, are gaining importance in Costa Rica's export market.

COFFEE AND MORE!

Since the 1800s, coffee has been a major source of revenue for Costa Rica. Coffee produced in the highland regions of the country is famous all over the world for its pure, rich taste.
(A Closer Look, page 54)

Left: **The vast grasslands of Guanacaste are ideal for raising cattle.**

Raw materials for industry, transportation, fuels, and construction make up the bulk of Costa Rica's imports. In 1996, Costa Rica suffered a U.S. $340 million trade deficit, meaning the country imported more goods than it exported. In an effort to expand both its export and import markets, Costa Rica offers tax incentives and other special concessions to companies that make non-traditional products.

Tourism

The tourism industry is one of Costa Rica's primary sources of revenue. About 700,000 people visit the country every year. In 1995, the industry generated U.S. $661 million.

The Workforce

More than a million people make up Costa Rica's workforce. Of this figure, 2 percent are employed in the government sector, 17 percent in industry, and 22 percent in agriculture. The majority of people, some 50 percent, are employed in the service sector. Services include social, financial, and personal services in the areas of health care, transportation, hotels, and real estate. In 1998, the unemployment rate in the country was 5.6 percent.

BANANAS

Minor Cooper Keith started banana cultivation in Costa Rica when he planted bananas by the side of the Atlantic Railway track to finance the railway's construction. Bananas soon became an important export crop.
(A Closer Look, page 46)

People and Lifestyle

Population Makeup

Although Costa Rica has a few minority groups, such as Afro-Costa Ricans, native Indians, Chinese, Italians, and Germans, its population is generally homogeneous. Since about 97 percent of Costa Ricans are white or mestizo, Costa Ricans are lighter skinned than their Central American neighbors. Costa Ricans refer to themselves as *Ticos* (TEE-kohs), a nickname that denotes the friendly and outgoing qualities of the Costa Rican people. *Tico* is also a suffix that Costa Ricans add to words.

Minority Groups

Afro-Costa Ricans make up the country's largest minority group. They descended from Jamaican workers who immigrated to the country in the late 1800s, and they still maintain their Jamaican culture today. Afro-Costa Ricans live on the Caribbean coast and speak English instead of Spanish.

Another minority group, the native Indians, lived in Costa Rica long before the arrival of Spanish settlers. With a population

GUANACASTE: BEACHES AND BEEF

Located in the northwestern part of Costa Rica, Guanacaste has an atmosphere that is quite different from the rest of the country. Cowboys and open plains characterize this province.
(*A Closer Look, page 60*)

Below: The Plaza de la Cultura in San José is a popular meeting place. People come here to visit the numerous shops, museums, and cafés or simply to sit and watch the bustle of activities.

of about 10,000, these indigenous peoples now constitute less than 3 percent of the country's population. They live near the southern border, most of them making a living as subsistence farmers. Chinese and retirees from the United States and Europe are other minority groups.

Above: This Indian family lives in a remote part of Costa Rica. Many of the indigenous peoples live in isolated communities in the highlands and along both coasts.

Meseta Central

More than two-thirds of Costa Ricans live in the Meseta Central, the central valley of Costa Rica, although this region accounts for only 5 percent of the country's total land area. The Meseta Central includes the capital city of San José and the smaller cities of Alajuela, Heredia, and Cartago.

Costa Rica has a narrower gap between rich and poor than many Latin American countries. Although it has a small elite class, and poverty exists, the middle class is large and well-educated. Regional inequality is a big problem in the country, with rural areas, such as the coasts and the northwestern Guanacaste province, having higher rates of unemployment than urban areas.

SAN JOSÉ: CAPITAL CITY

San José is the cultural center of Costa Rica and the hub of a thriving agricultural area. It is the largest city in Costa Rica, with a population of about one million people. San José's history goes as far back as 1737.

(A Closer Look, page 66)

21

Family Life

Costa Ricans believe in the importance of family, and most of the people work hard to establish and keep their families together. The divorce rate, however, is high in Costa Rica, and many births occur outside of marriage. About 14,000 teenage pregnancies take place in Costa Rica every year.

About 20 percent of all Costa Rican households are run by single mothers, without fathers to help raise children or provide income. Married women, however, suffer other kinds of hardships. For example, Costa Rica's Ministry of Health has reported that spousal abuse is a problem in the country. Through education and counseling, Costa Rican authorities are working to reduce incidences of marital abuse.

"Queen Bee" Family

A typical rural family structure in Costa Rica is the "Queen Bee" family, in which women not only run the household but also provide the only source of income. Grandmothers look after the children, while mothers work for a living.

Below: **Costa Rican women are expected to be more responsible for their families than men. This attitude is slowly changing.**

Men, Women, *Machismo*, and *Marianismo*

Above: **From youth, men are taught to be brave and aggressive and to engage in sports and manly activities, such as repairing cars.**

Machismo (mah-CHEES-moh) is the idea that men are superior to women. It is a common attitude in many Latin American countries and comes through in the politics, culture, and everyday life of Costa Rica. Men are expected to be "macho" and daring. They do little housework and receive many privileges in society because of their gender.

Marianismo (mah-ree-ahn-EES-moh) is the attitude that female behavior should emphasize self-sacrifice. The concept of physical beauty is also strongly stressed. Women are seen as objects of beauty to be admired. They are expected to do household chores and serve their husbands or boyfriends. Because women are brought up to believe that suffering makes them better people, the best compliment they can receive is to be called *abnegado* (ahb-nay-GAH-doh), or self-sacrificing.

For the most part, relationships in Costa Rica tend to follow machismo/marianismo patterns, especially in rural areas. Although women are gaining more respect in the workforce, they still have obstacles to overcome in society at large.

Education

The literacy rate in Costa Rica has improved over the past century. In 1920, only 50 percent of the population was literate, but, by 1973, that number had risen to 89 percent. Today, Costa Rica boasts a literacy rate of 94.8 percent, the highest in Central America.

Costa Rica made education free and compulsory in 1886. It was one of the first countries in the world to do so. Today, children must attend school until the age of fourteen.

Above: **After school, children in a primary school in Costa Rica have fun on slides.**

Higher Learning

The University of Costa Rica opened in 1940 in San José. It is the oldest university in the country and has an enrollment of 35,000 students. Costa Rica has three other state-funded institutions of higher learning: the National University of Heredia, the Technical Institute of Costa Rica in Cartago, and the State Correspondence University. The country is also home to the University for Peace, a school sponsored by the United Nations.

Costa Rica has about one hundred libraries, where students and adults can read their favorite novels or magazines and keep up with the latest information about technological advancements.

FRANKLIN CHANG DIAZ

Costa Rican-born Franklin Chang Diaz was the first Latin American astronaut to travel into space. Between 1986 and 1998, he flew in six Space Shuttle missions and spent more than 1,269 hours in space.

(A Closer Look, page 50)

Problems to Overcome

Compared to other countries in Central America, Costa Rica has an excellent education system. It is, however, not without problems. For example, the system is often criticized for not having enough adequately trained teachers. This problem is more severe in rural areas. Teaching is not an attractive career option in these areas because teachers are poorly paid and have a low status in society. Furthermore, classrooms are overcrowded, with up to forty students squeezed into one room.

Many Costa Ricans think the national syllabus is outdated and students are not getting enough practical experience in the classroom. The high drop-out rate among students is another major concern.

Government Response

Recognizing the need to improve the education system, the government, in 1997, acknowledged problems by setting aside 22 percent of the government budget, a substantial increase over previous years, for education.

Below: **A group of university students takes a break between their classes.**

Religion

The 1949 constitution states that Roman Catholicism is the national religion of Costa Rica. It also guarantees the freedom of religious practice to all other Christian denominations.

The Catholic Church is considered the basis of Costa Rican society's beliefs, policies, and practices. More than 90 percent of the population is Roman Catholic. Catholics here are generally more relaxed about religious practices than their Central American counterparts. Less than 20 percent of Costa Rican Catholics, for example, attend church regularly. Women, however, attend mass more regularly than men. Also, despite its Catholic heritage, Costa Rica legalized divorce in 1974.

Semana Santa

Holy Week, or *Semana Santa* (say-MAHN-ah SAHN-tah), is a national holiday in Costa Rica and takes place in spring. Large celebrations are held throughout the week, and thousands of people participate in the festivities. The highlights of Holy Week are the processions that wind through towns and cities.

Below: Eating, drinking, and dancing follow a typical Costa Rican church wedding.

Praying to Saints

Catholic saints and the Virgin Mary play big roles in Costa Rican society. People often pray to their favorite saints for help or guidance in their daily lives.

Every year, on August 2, thousands of people from all over Costa Rica make a pilgrimage to Cartago to visit the Cartago Basilica and pay homage to the *Virgen de los Angeles* (VAIR-hen day lohs AHN-hail-ays), who has been the patron saint of Costa Rica since 1782.

Above: **The beautiful Cartago Basilica contains a statue of Costa Rica's patron saint, the Virgen de los Angeles.**

Protestant Faiths

Protestant religions are on the rise in Costa Rica. Currently, about 40,000 Costa Ricans, the majority of whom are Afro-Costa Ricans, are Protestants. Evangelical churches, which emphasize the Bible's importance and a personal belief in Christ for finding salvation, are gaining influence. Other Protestant groups in Costa Rica include Methodists, Baptists, and Pentecostals.

Language and Literature

Spanish is the national language of Costa Rica, but the Costa Rican dialect is slightly different from the Castilian dialect spoken in Spain. The biggest difference between these two Spanish dialects is the use of *tú*, meaning "you." In Castilian Spanish and other Spanish dialects spoken around the world, such as in Mexico and Argentina, *tú* is a familiar term used to address close friends. *Usted* and *vos,* two other words meaning "you," are used in more formal situations with superiors and elders. In Costa Rica, however, the *tú* form of "you" is not used at all. Costa Ricans use *usted* and *vos,* instead.

Suffixes

Across Latin America, people tend to create diminutives by adding the suffix *ito*. Spanish spoken in Costa Rica, however, uses the suffix *tico*. For example, the word *pato* (PAH-toe), which means "duck" in Spanish, becomes *patico* (pah-TEE-coh), or "little duck," in Costa Rican Spanish, instead of the Latin American *patito* (pah-TEE-toe).

Below: **Although Spanish is the official language of Costa Rica, English is also widely spoken. Because of the large numbers of English-speaking immigrants and tourists, many Costa Ricans speak and understand English. For English-speaking tourists in Costa Rica, signs at popular places of interest are displayed in English as well in as Spanish.**

Literature

The most significant feature of Costa Rican literature is its *costumbrismo* (koh-stoom-BREES-moh), or local color. Novelists, essayists, and short-story writers often portray the lives of peasants and agricultural workers in local settings. One such essayist from the first half of the twentieth century was Joaquín García Monge. García edited *El Repertorio Americano,* or *American Repertory*, a magazine that received rave reviews for its intellectual and literary value. García also wrote what most believe to be the first important Costa Rican novel, *El Moto*, published in 1900.

A movement that started in the 1940s left an indelible mark on Costa Rica's literary scene. Its core group of authors — Joaquín Gutiérrez, Fabián Dobles, Carlos Salazar Herrera, and Carlos Luis Fallas — focused on social realism and social themes of the time. The most influential work created by a member of this group was *Mamita Yunai*, written by Carlos Luis Fallas in 1941. This book describes the squalid living and working conditions on banana plantations. *Mamita Yunai* is still required reading in Costa Rican schools.

Contemporary authors who address social concerns in their novels include Alberto Camas, Tatiana Lobo Wiehoff, and Anacristina Rossi.

Arts

Costa Rica is home to artists who practice both traditional and modern art forms. San José is the base for many of these artists. Costa Rican crafts include jewelry, reproductions of pre-Columbian pottery, and woodcarvings, particularly the carved masks worn by the indigenous peoples of the south.

Oxcarts

Colorful oxcarts, or *carretas* (kah-RAY-tahs), have become a national symbol of Costa Rica. The oxcarts come in all sizes and feature detailed, brightly painted designs.

The tradition of painting oxcarts began almost one hundred years ago. Oxcarts were originally used to transport harvested coffee beans from the fields to the coast, where the beans were shipped abroad. At the beginning of the twentieth century, local artists from the town of Sarchí, less than an hour's drive from San José, began to paint the oxcarts, with unique designs for each

Below: **Elaborately painted oxcarts are a specialty of Sarchí, a town northeast of San José. These oxcarts are displayed in parades and exhibitions across the country.**

region. By looking at the designs, people were able to identify the area from which each oxcart originated.

Above: **Day of the Oxcart Drivers features oxcarts and cowboys.**

The Tradition Continues

Oxcarts are still made and painted today in Sarchí, the crafts capital of Costa Rica. The carts are painted from wheels to sideboards, and the colorful designs that decorate them can be found all over Sarchí, from the facade of a local church to windows and doors of homes to garbage cans. Many tourists buy miniature oxcarts as souvenirs. Using the fine-tipped brushes of oxcart artists, tourists sometimes even paint the carts themselves.

Celebrating the Beauty of Oxcarts

Every year, an oxcart festival called *Día de los Boyeros* (DEE-ah day lohs boy-AIR-ohs), which means Day of the Oxcart Drivers, takes place in the mountain town of San Antonio de Escazú, located near San José. This festival is celebrated on the second Sunday of March, and thousands of people flock to the town to watch colorful oxcart parades. Usually, more than one hundred oxcart drivers take part in the parades.

Nicoya Pottery

The small town of Guaitíl on the Nicoya Peninsula is well known for Nicoya pottery. Dating back to the pre-Columbian era, the Chorotega Indians, who once inhabited the Nicoya Peninsula in great numbers, left behind a legacy of ceramics, including plates, bowls, incense burners, and animal and human figurines. The tradition of creating this pottery has survived to this day.

Unique Designs

Nicoya pottery was produced in the northwestern region of Costa Rica in A.D. 500–1000. This pottery is known for its bright, colorful designs. To create the ceramics, potters used molding and coiling techniques, rolling clay into coils before shaping it, and decorated the pieces in red, black, orange, yellow, maroon, and cream colors. Although the art of creating Nicoya pottery was not practiced for centuries, today, women in Guaitíl are reviving the art. They dig their own clay from nearby hills and create beautiful ceramic pieces in the tradition of the original pottery.

Below: **Guaitíl's traditional pottery is one of Costa Rica's most popular folk art purchases.**

Music and Dance

Costa Ricans have a deep love for music and dance. Ticos are always ready to hit the dance floor or attend a concert. They swing to the sounds of pop music in local bars and discotheques, and dance close together to the beat of a samba.

The *punto guanacasteco* (POON-toh gwon-ah-kass-TAY-koh) is the national dance of Costa Rica. Couples do this folk dance to guitar music during special events and traditional exhibitions. The punto guanacasteco involves a lot of stomping.

Above: **Dancers in colorful costumes perform a fast-paced folk dance.**

Classical Music

The National Symphony Orchestra of Costa Rica is an artistic outlet for classical music lovers. Before 1970, it was a small orchestra that performed a few concerts a year. In the 1970s, Gerald Brown, an American, revitalized it, and the orchestra has been prosperous ever since. Over the years, the National Theater, located in the heart of San José, has been the home of the symphony orchestra. Each year, talented conductors and popular singers and soloists from around the world have performed with the National Symphony Orchestra to sellout crowds.

Leisure and Festivals

Costa Ricans spend their leisure time in a wide variety of ways, from playing sports to attending cultural events. In urban areas, people like to see American movies, eat out at restaurants, and visit with family and friends. On weekends, music lovers go where they can hear bands playing their favorite songs, or they visit the National Theater to listen to the National Symphony Orchestra. Costa Rican theater companies perform highly entertaining comedy, drama, or mime productions, of both international and local origins. Every March, arts festivals feature dance, theater, and music from around the world.

The Great Outdoors

Costa Ricans enjoy their country's national parks as much as tourists do. Thirty-five parks are spread all over the country, making them easily accessible to everyone. Many Costa Ricans visit their national parks on weekends and national holidays.

NATIONAL PARKS

The natural splendor of Costa Rica's national parks is a major tourist attraction. The Costa Rican government is making many efforts to protect the land.
(*A Closer Look, page 63*)

Left: **Cafés and small restaurants abound in Costa Rica. Eating out is a fun and inexpensive way to spend time with friends.**

The National Theater

Theater is popular in Costa Rica, and some believe that the country has more theater companies than any other country in the world. Drama became part of the Costa Rican school curriculum in the early twentieth century and further boosted the popularity of the dramatic arts.

Theater companies often perform in the National Theater, a cultural center for Costa Rica. The National Theater's construction was partially funded by the coffee barons of the nineteenth century. The remaining funds came from taxes paid by the local people. This lavishly decorated building is a symbol of pride among Costa Ricans.

Earthquake Scare

Since the National Theater opened on October 21, 1897, hundreds of people have performed there. In 1965, it was declared a national monument. Less than thirty years later, in 1991, an earthquake severely damaged the theater. A nationwide fund-raiser brought in enough money to pay for repairs.

Sports

Costa Ricans have a love of sports that is reflected in their culture and surroundings. With beautiful, warm weather all year, Costa Ricans are especially fond of outdoor sports. Spectator sports include soccer, tennis, and bicycle races. Another favorite sport is bullfighting, which, in Costa Rica, is more of a game than a fight. The matador teases and slaps the bull, then scrambles to safety when the animal charges.

Playing with Balls

Basketball courts and soccer fields dot major cities and rural villages across the country. Soccer is, by far, the most popular sport in the country. Every town, small or large, has at least one soccer team. Major cities and bigger towns have stadiums for soccer and other games. The country's most popular soccer team is from San José and is called Saprissa, but nicknamed *El Monstro*, or the Monster. Baseball is popular in the city of Limón, where private organizations fund teams.

FISHING

The warm, tropical waters off Costa Rica are ideal for fishing. Marlins, tarpon, and sailfish put up a good fight, luring fishing enthusiasts from around the world.
(*A Closer Look, page 58*)

Below: **Every village in Costa Rica has a soccer field, and matches between rival teams take place frequently.**

Water Sports

People travel from all over the world to experience the wonders of Costa Rica's oceans and rivers. The country's two coastlines are excellent places for the adventurous to test their limits against the elements. Scuba diving, surfing, fishing, rafting, kayaking, and snorkeling are some of the many water sports gaining popularity in the country.

Windsurfers' brightly colored sails glide across the waters of Lake Arenal in northern Costa Rica, one of the finest locations for windsurfers to pit their skills against each other. Gusty winds all year long make for ideal windsurfing conditions. Although windsurfers frequent Lake Arenal, the surrounding area is still too undeveloped for the area to be popular.

White-Water Rafting

Costa Rica has some of the most accessible rivers and rapids in the world for white-water rafting. Local companies provide services for three- or four-day tours on rivers. Rafting conditions range from beginner to expert. The slower currents on beginner routes allow rafters to take in Costa Rica's rich, tropical plant life as they travel down rivers.

Above: **White-water rafting is new to Costa Rica but is growing in popularity. The country's geography lends itself well to this sport.**

Festivals

Most festivals in Costa Rica are religious. Each town in the country has its own patron saint, who is honored with a celebration every year. The country's patron saint, the Virgen de Los Angeles, is honored with a national holiday on August 2.

Christmas

Christmas is a special time in Costa Rica. People begin celebrating this holiday in late November, first putting up decorations, and later displaying their Christmas trees. Some Costa Ricans send greeting cards to family, friends, and colleagues.

Nativity Scene

Although Christmas celebrations in Costa Rica are becoming more commercialized every year, they still include a truly Costa Rican tradition. Each family sets up a nativity scene, either under their Christmas tree or on a table. On Christmas Eve, they add baby Jesus to the scene. Costa Rican children believe the baby Jesus brings them gifts during the night of Christmas Eve.

CARNIVAL LIMÓN

The city of Limón comes to life in October for an annual carnival that celebrates Columbus's landing in Costa Rica on September 18, 1502. Included in the carnival's activities are games, sports, and crafts.
(A Closer Look, page 48)

Left: **Thousands of people gather in Cartago to watch the traditional procession of the Virgen de los Angeles.**

Adults usually open their presents on Christmas Eve, but children must wait until Christmas Day.

Beginning December 15, in a Christian tradition called *posadas* (poh-SAH-dahs), neighbors visit each other's homes to recreate the journey of Joseph and Mary to Bethlehem. They pray, eat, and sing carols to celebrate the Christmas season and offer thanks to God. Many Costa Ricans take leave from work the week between Christmas and New Year's Day.

The Mango Festival

Every year in July, the Mango Festival is held in the town of Alajuela, just northwest of San José. This nine-day festival features arts and crafts fairs, parades, food, and music.

Independence Day

Costa Ricans celebrate Independence Day on September 15, the day in 1821 that Costa Rica and the rest of Central America were proclaimed free from Spanish rule. Today, Independence Day is celebrated with colorful parades all over the country. At night, children carry lighted lanterns along a special path to celebrate their freedom.

Above: **On September 9, Costa Ricans celebrate Children's Day, a school holiday when children take part in parades, dances, and other fun activities. This day leads up to festivities for Independence Day on September 15.**

SEMANA SANTA

Costa Rica's Catholic community celebrates Semana Santa, or Holy Week, with beautiful processions. On the Saturday before Easter, they celebrate Judas Day, a festival in contrast with the somber mood of Semana Santa.

(A Closer Look, page 70)

Food

Rice, beans, and maize are the basic staples of the Costa Rican diet and are included in most meals, from breakfast to dinner. A typical breakfast dish is *gallo pinto* (GUY-yoh PEEN-toh), or "spotted rooster." This dish consists of black beans and rice seasoned with onions and spices.

A popular dish served during lunch is *casado* (cah-SAH-doh), which is rice served with beans, eggs, meat, and vegetables. Another favorite, *arroz con pollo* (arr-ROHS kohn POH-yoh), consists of chicken and rice. Sometimes, it is served with seafood, such as shrimp, octopus, or squid, instead of chicken.

Fruits Galore

Costa Rica is a haven for fruit lovers. Exotic fruits, such as papayas, litchis, starfruit, pineapples, guavas, passion fruit, coco plums, rambutans, rose apples, star apples, and loquats, are found there in abundance.

Left: **The streets surrounding San José's central market are lined with fresh produce.**

Beverages

Coffee is a popular drink in Costa Rica because the economy was built on it. In San José, the aroma of roasting coffee is everywhere. Another popular drink is *agua dulce* (AH-gwah DOOL-say), or sweet water. It is nothing more than brown sugar mixed into boiling water.

In some parts of Costa Rica, especially along the coasts, people drink coconut milk right out of the coconuts. A customer selects a coconut, and the coconut vendor slices an opening in the top of the nut with a machete. The customer drinks the refreshing coconut milk through the opening, sometimes using a straw.

Bocas

Costa Ricans love to snack, and small snacks, called *bocas* (BOH-cahs), are served at many cafés and restaurants. Bocas, also called *boquitas* (boh-KEE-tahs), may include soup, chicken wings, or potato chips. Other common bocas are *tortillas con queso* (tor-TEE-ahs kohn KAY-soh), tortillas with cheese; *ceviche* (say-VEE-chay), fish marinated in spices and juices for hours and then served raw; and *huevos de tortuga* (HUAY-vohs day tor-TOO-gah), turtle eggs.

A CLOSER LOOK AT COSTA RICA

Costa Rica's natural beauty and diverse animal life are the country's major attractions. The quetzal, a mystical bird, and the sea turtle, both endangered species, are indigenous to Costa Rica. The country has lush tropical vegetation, and its fertile soil produces coffee and bananas for export. Its diverse fresh- and saltwater ecosystems are delights for anglers and nature lovers.

The National Parks System, established in 1970, protects Costa Rica's population of birds and other animals, as well as its forests. Many active and inactive volcanoes, which characterize the landscape of Costa Rica, are found in these national parks.

Several aspects of Costa Rican culture set it apart from the rest of Central America. The most notable of these is the country's policy of peace. José Figueres, the grandfather of modern Costa Rica, was instrumental in establishing the democracy that Costa Rica enjoys to this day.

Opposite: **This group's lively dance steps keep spectators enthralled during Carnival Limón.**

Below: **Music is a part of most celebrations in Costa Rica.**

The Atlantic Railway

Without the perseverance of the nineteenth-century coffee barons, the Atlantic Railway that connects the Meseta Central to the Caribbean coast would never have been built.

In the nineteenth century, coffee was transported by oxcart from the Meseta Central to the Caribbean coast, then sent to Europe on ships. The coffee barons realized they needed a more efficient way to get coffee beans to the coast. Building a railway was the answer. They selected the city of Limón as the final destination for the new railway and the site for a new port.

Minor Cooper Keith

In 1872, construction on the railway began under the supervision of an American by the name of Minor Cooper Keith. A British bank funded this huge project, providing Costa Rica with a loan of U.S. $3 million. The railway track was to run from San José, where the coffee was grown, to Limón, where it would be exported. Keith brought workers from around the world, including Jamaicans, Italians, and Chinese, to help construct

Left: **The Atlantic Railway, also known as the "Jungle Train," is 120 miles (193 km) long.**

the railway. Today, Costa Rica's black population traces its roots to the Jamaican workers employed by Keith. Working conditions were tough, and over 4,000 people died during the construction phase of the project. In 1890, eighteen years after the project began, the railroad was completed.

Above: **Until early 1970, the Atlantic Railway was the only existing travel route between the Meseta Central and the city of Limón.**

Keith realized the potential of the land along both sides of the railway. He believed it would be ideal for banana plantations. In 1884, Keith took responsibility for the debt Costa Rica owed the British bank. In exchange, he was given a 99-year lease on huge areas of land along the Atlantic Railway route, free use of the railway once it was completed, and a twenty-year tax postponement. Keith's business venture was successful. He established plantations on his land, and, in 1899, he founded the United Fruit Company. Soon, bananas were exported from the port of Limón.

The Atlantic Railway proved to be an excellent way of transporting coffee to the port. For people in rural areas, it was also a mode of transportation from the countryside to San José. In 1991, an earthquake forced the closure of some parts of the Atlantic Railway. Trains still run in the Caribbean lowlands, but they no longer run through the mountains.

Bananas

Important Export Crop

Bananas are important exports of Costa Rica. The province of
Limón is home to many banana plantations. In 1995, Costa Rica
exported U.S. $580 million worth of bananas, making bananas the
second most profitable industry in the country, after tourism's
U.S. $661 million earnings.

Today, Costa Rica is one of the largest producers of bananas
in the world. The banana industry was set up more than a
hundred years ago by American Minor Cooper Keith, who
founded the United Fruit Company in 1899. Another banana
company, the Standard Fruit Company, was established about
sixty-five years later. Today, these two multinational companies,

Left: **A plantation
worker checks the
condition of the
ripening bananas.**

46

now called Chiquita Brands and Standard Fruit/Dole, together with Del Monte, account for nearly all the production, distribution, and export of bananas. Smaller local companies produce bananas for the domestic market.

Above: **Bananas make up one-fifth of Costa Rica's total exports. The banana industry employs about 50,000 people, including plantation workers, sorters, and sellers.**

Concerns to Address

Although exporting bananas is a huge source of revenue for Costa Rica, the banana industry has a number of problems. Bananas are susceptible to disease. To fight diseases, companies must use large amounts of insecticide, which, in turn, pose a health threat to plantation workers. Another problem is finding land for growing bananas. Clearing large areas of land for banana plantations leads to deforestation. Costa Rica is working hard to keep its forests intact, but banana plantations are springing up fast. Low wages, the use of illegal workers, and poor working conditions are other problems.

In 1993, the European Union (EU) set quotas on banana imports so that no single country could decrease its banana prices to beat competition from another country. Each country has a fixed number on the quantity of bananas it may export to EU countries. This ruling caused a furor in Costa Rica, and, more than six years later, it is still under debate.

Carnival Limón

The port city of Limón, home to about 65,000 people, becomes the center of attention every year when it hosts Carnival Limón. This carnival is similar to one held in Rio de Janeiro, Brazil, but it takes place on a much smaller scale. Thousands of people, both Costa Ricans and tourists, take part in the festivities, many traveling great distances to join the big celebration. Carnival Limón takes place every October and lasts almost an entire week.

Celebrating Columbus's Landing

Carnival Limón commemorates Christopher Columbus's landing in Costa Rica on September 18, 1502. Also called *Día de las Culturas* (DEE-ah day lahs kool-TOO-rahs), or the Day of Cultures, the festival celebrates this day of "discovery" in a Mardi Gras atmosphere. The province's large Jamaican population is reflected in the Carnival's many Caribbean influences, such as dancing to the catchy strains of Caribbean music. Wild revelers,

Below: **Children in bright costumes add color and excitement to the Carnival parade.**

lively bands, and breathtaking fireworks make Carnival Limón a truly exciting event.

Above: **A crowd gathers to watch couples do the salsa, a popular dance form in Latin America.**

Fun for All

Carnival Limón begins on Tuesday and offers entertainment and activities throughout the week, until Sunday. Restaurants stay open 24 hours a day, and, on the streets, food and drink stands enjoy good business from hungry and thirsty revelers.

Carnivalgoers can watch bullfights, take part in dance contests, or learn how to make traditional crafts from skilled artisans. There are competitions of various kinds for both children and adults. One of the most popular events is a beauty contest to select the Carnival Queen. Hundreds of young women take part in this contest.

The Parade

The highlight of Carnival Limón is the parade, a procession of hundreds of people dressed in colorful costumes. As the procession makes its way through the streets, bystanders dance along. Loud music fills the air, and everyone has a lot of fun.

Franklin Chang Diaz

Franklin Chang Diaz is the highest-ranking Latin American in the United States space program. He has the distinct honor of being the first Costa Rican, and the first Latin American, astronaut to travel in space.

Chang Diaz was born April 5, 1950, in San José, Costa Rica. His family moved to Venezuela after he was born, but they later returned to Costa Rica. After finishing high school in Costa Rica, Chang Diaz worked in a local bank to earn money, so he could continue his studies in the United States. Within a year, he moved to Connecticut where, to improve his English, he repeated his senior year of high school.

Chang Diaz won a scholarship to the University of Connecticut, and, in 1973, he received a bachelor's degree in mechanical engineering. Later, he won another scholarship to study at the Massachusetts Institute of Technology (MIT). At MIT, he earned a doctorate in applied plasma physics.

Left: **Franklin Chang Diaz won six NASA Space Flight Medals in 1986, 1989, 1992, 1994, 1996, and 1998; two NASA Distinguished Service Medals in 1995 and 1997; and three NASA Exceptional Service Medals in 1988, 1990, and 1993.**

Left: **Franklin Chang Diaz and his colleague, Janet Kavandi, participate in the Crew Equipment Interface Test, or CEIT, at NASA's Orbit Processing Facility.**

Chang Diaz became a U.S. citizen in 1980, after living in the United States for more than ten years. That same year, he applied for an astronaut position at the National Aeronautics and Space Administration (NASA). Although there were more than 4,000 applicants for only nineteen astronaut positions, Chang Diaz was selected to be part of the prestigious NASA program.

On January 12, 1986, Chang Diaz joined the crew of the Space Shuttle *Columbia* for his first space mission. On board the *Columbia*, he observed Halley's Comet up close and conducted tests on the ozone layer. By June 1998, Chang Diaz had completed five more space missions. With more than 1,269 hours in space, he is the U.S. astronaut with the highest rate of participation in Space Shuttle missions.

In April 1995, Costa Rica honored Chang Diaz with its "Honorary Citizen" award. Today, Chang Diaz works in the Advanced Space Propulsion Laboratory at NASA. He is researching an ion engine for the Space Shuttle, which would cut the time of a manned mission to Mars from a projected three years to just seven months.

Cocos Island

The Largest Uninhabited Island

Cocos Island is located about 360 miles (579 km) south of Puntarenas in the Pacific Ocean. Formed by a volcanic eruption, this isolated island covers an area of 15 square miles (39 square km). Cocos Island is the largest uninhabited island in the world and the only island in the eastern Pacific with rain forests. It is a protected national park with more than two hundred waterfalls and many species of plants and animals. Its clear waters and teeming coral reefs make it one of the best scuba-diving sites in the world.

The Spaniards sighted Cocos Island in 1526. Sixteen years later, the French named the island *Ile de Coques*, which means Nutshell or Shell Island. The Spaniards misinterpreted this name and called the island Cocos Island, or Island of the Coconut. "Island of the Eternal Rains" might have been a more appropriate name, since the island receives more than 288 inches (732 centimeters) of rain a year.

According to some legends, several pirate treasures are buried on Cocos Island. The Devonshire Treasure, the treasure of Benito Bonito, and the Great Treasure of Lima are all rumored to be hidden here. The modern-day value of these treasures is said to be over U.S. $500 million. Several fortune hunters have gone to Cocos Island in search of gold, silver, and jewels, but, so far, no one has been successful.

Sharks and Movies

Professional divers come to Cocos Island, even though the island is well-known for the large number of sharks swimming in waters surrounding it. Schools of hammerhead sharks are a common sight, as are silky, whitetip, and blacktip sharks. Dolphins and whales are also found here.

Underwater filmmakers Howard and Michele Hall spent 450 hours in the waters off Cocos Island to film *Island of the Sharks*, which was released in 1999. The Halls' production drew attention to the shark-infested waters of Cocos Island. They shot 300 rolls of film, each capturing three minutes of footage and each costing U.S. $3,000 to process and develop.

Above: **Canadian writer Margaret Atwood holds a picture of a newly discovered species of weevil found only on Cocos Island. This species will bear her family name, in honor of her father, Dr. Carl Atwood (1906–1993), a conservationist.**

Opposite: **Chatham Bay is one of Cocos Island's two natural harbors. The other is Wafer Bay. Both bays are located on the northern coast of the island.**

Coffee and More!

A Popular Beverage

Costa Rica produces some of the best coffee beans in the world. With over 2,500 different varieties of coffee available in the country, it is a popular drink among Costa Ricans. Coffee was introduced to Europe a few hundred years ago and has become so popular that it is now a regular part of people's diets.

Coffee in the New World

In the 1700s, European travelers brought coffee from Arabia and Ethiopia to the New World. In 1779, the first coffee bushes were planted and harvested in the Meseta Central of Costa Rica. The fertile soil of the Meseta Central, along with Costa Rica's climate, provided ideal conditions for this new crop.

Coffee bushes were planted on large plots of land, called *fincas* (FEEN-cuhz). As crops were harvested, the finca owners became wealthy, and a coffee elite emerged. By 1830, coffee had become a large source of revenue for Costa Rica. In 1849, a member of the coffee elite, Juan Rafael Mora Porras, became president of Costa Rica.

Below: **Coffee plantations in Costa Rica provide jobs for many people.**

Left: Coffee beans are among Costa Rica's leading exports.

Opportunity knocked for Costa Rica's coffee industry in 1843, when an empty ship bound for England stopped in Costa Rica. The ship needed bulky materials to steady its load, so Costa Ricans filled it with bags of coffee, and the ship set sail for England. Coffee became a huge success in Great Britain, opening up the European market to Costa Rica's coffee exporters.

Below: Few visitors to Costa Rica leave the country without buying several packages of coffee.

The coffee industry continued to expand throughout the 1800s and 1900s. During this time, growing and exporting coffee were profitable, but not without problems. The worldwide economic crisis of 1929, and, later, World War II, brought about big drops in coffee prices. As the supply of coffee exceeded its demand, coffee prices dropped even further. Costa Rica was forced to endure many years of low coffee exports and a weak economy.

Today, the coffee industry is one of the biggest employers in Costa Rica. Workers handpick coffee berries during the harvest season, which runs from November through January. Although coffee was the country's biggest export in the past, the banana industry has recently surpassed it in terms of revenue.

José Figueres

José Figueres Ferrer, affectionately known as Don Pepe, was born September 25, 1906, in San Ramón, Alajuela. He received his early and tertiary education in Costa Rica, then left for the United States to further his studies at MIT. He returned to Costa Rica in the 1920s and soon became a member of the coffee elite. In 1942, he was exiled to Mexico for two years, as punishment for criticizing the government and labeling it corrupt.

In 1948, many dramatic changes took place in Costa Rican politics. In the national elections that year, presidential candidate Otilio Ulate Blanco emerged victorious, but President Rafael Angel Calderón Guardia declared the results null and void. As Calderón and his followers tried to prevent the installation of the Ulate government, Costa Rica suffered two months of civil war. Figueres opposed Calderón's policies and led an uprising against the rebels. On April 18, 1948, when the rebel forces surrendered, Figueres took power.

Left: **José Figueres was president of Costa Rica for several terms. He outlined four goals for Costa Rica that govern its character to this day: honesty in the government, liberty for the people, professionalism in public administration, and government guidance in the economy for a fair distribution of wealth.**

Left: José Figueres and his wife made an official three-day visit to London in 1956 as part of a European tour.

New Constitution

Figueres led a junta, a military government that takes power by force, for eighteen months in Costa Rica. Under the junta, the Constitution of 1949 was written. This constitution, which is still in use today, abolished the army and gave women the right to vote. After stabilizing the political situation in Costa Rica, Figueres gave up power in 1949. Ulate succeeded him.

In 1951, Figueres formed the PLN, and, in the 1953 election, he was elected president. Figueres served a four-year term and became known for his anti-Communist, anti-dictatorship stand. He was a firm believer in democracy and instituted many social and economic reforms, including giving control of the banks and insurance companies to the government.

Carrying the Torch

Figueres served as president again from 1970 to 1974. He died in San José on June 8, 1990, at the age of eighty-three, but his legacy continued when his son, José María Figueres Olsen, served as president of Costa Rica from 1994 to 1998. José Figueres will always be fondly remembered as the grandfather of democracy in Costa Rica.

Fishing

A Perfect Setting

Costa Rica's long coastlines, along with its many rivers and lakes, make it a perfect setting for fishing. Fishing enthusiasts can choose from hundreds of charter services and personal guides to help them find and catch both fresh- and saltwater fish, as well as rent boats and fishing equipment.

The Caribbean and Pacific coasts offer excellent sites for fishing. Barra del Colorado, on the northeastern Caribbean coast, is a major fishing area. Because it is not easily accessible by land, visitors must travel there by boat or plane. Flamingo Beach, on the northern Pacific coast, and Tamarindo Beach, on the northwestern Pacific coast, are also popular fishing destinations.

Knowing When and Where to Fish

Sailfish, tarpon, marlins, snook, wahoos, roosterfish, and snappers, among others, swim in the waters off Costa Rica.

Left: **Fishing with a bow and arrow is an interesting alternative to the rod and reel.**

Above: **This satisfied fisherman shows off his catch.**

Some of these fish, such as tarpon and snook, can live in both fresh- and saltwater, so they thrive in rivers and lakes, as well as in the ocean. Fishing conditions in Costa Rica vary depending on the type of fish, the time of year, and the location. For example, conditions are excellent, November through April, for hooking Pacific sailfish in Quepos, located along the Pacific coast. From May to July, conditions are good for catching black marlins on Flamingo Beach.

One of the most difficult fish to catch is the tarpon. This fish puts up a strong fight when hooked and can be reeled in only by experts. Sailfish, which are large, silvery fish with long fins running down their backs, are usually released right after they are caught, so others can enjoy the sport of catching them.

Fishing Policies

To protect certain kinds of fish, many charter companies enforce special fishing guidelines. Some companies ask their clients to throw back all of their catch; other companies have a "keep what you can eat" policy, which requires only the "extra" catch be thrown back into the water.

Guanacaste: Beaches and Beef

The Nicoya Peninsula

Guanacaste province is located in the northwestern corner of Costa Rica. It includes most of the Nicoya Peninsula and spreads northward and eastward until it reaches Nicaragua and the province of Alajuela.

The Nicoya Peninsula juts out into the Pacific Ocean and is a popular vacation spot for tourists and locals. It has beautiful beaches, some of them remote and inaccessible. Santa Cruz, with a population of 15,000, and Nicoya, with a population of 10,000, are the most popular cities on the peninsula.

History

Guanacaste was once part of Nicaragua, but the province seceded from that country in 1821 and, for a while, became a small, independent country wedged between Nicaragua and Costa Rica.

Below: **Although Guanacaste has fertile soil, its isolation has led to few people living in the province.**

People in Guanacaste voted to become part of Costa Rica, but the province remained independent until 1824, when it finally became part of Costa Rica. Guanacaste's capital is Liberia. The province's trademark, and Costa Rica's national tree, is the guanacaste, a tree nicknamed the "ear tree" because its seed pots resemble ears.

Above: **Constant hot weather and a shorter rainy season make Guanacaste ideal for water sports.**

Cattle and Cowboys

With many open plains and grasslands, cattle raising is popular in Guanacaste. *Sabaneros* (sah-bah-NAY-rohs), or cowboys, work on the ranches that dot the province. The Guanacaste climate tends to be dry most of the year, a stark contrast to the wet climate of the central highlands and Caribbean lowlands.

Las Pumas

A unique place to visit in Guanacaste is Las Pumas, a zoo established in 1967. This zoo, located near Cañas, is home to the big cats of Costa Rica. Here, cougars, ocelots, jaguars, and margays, all rescued from hunters' traps, are rehabilitated and nurtured back to health. The animals are not returned to the wild because, once domesticated, they lose some of their survival skills.

National Parks

Preserving the Environment

Costa Rica's National Parks System was established in 1970, with the founding of the Santa Rosa National Park. Today, there are thirty-five national parks in the country. Twelve percent of Costa Rica's land area is protected in its National Parks System. The Costa Rican government plans, eventually, to increase this parks system to cover 19 percent of its land. An additional 16 percent of the country is protected in a large system of forest reserves, indigenous reserves, regional parks, and heritage sites. In total, an area of more than 5,000 square miles (12,950 square km) is protected. Individuals and groups are also buying tracts of Costa Rica's wilderness for preservation

Opposite: **Waterfalls characterize many of Costa Rica's thirty-five national parks.**

Attractions

The national parks in Costa Rica encompass many different ecosystems, from coral reefs and swamplands to rain forests and cloud forests. Beautiful beaches, cascading waterfalls, underground caves, crystal lakes, and towering volcanoes are home to approximately 5 percent of the world's plant and animal species, including one thousand species of orchids and fifty thousand species of insects. The parks also support the scientific research of many environmentalists and conservationists.

Below: **Butterflies are part of the natural habitat of Manuel Antonio National Park along the Pacific coast.**

Tourism and Other Problems

In 1994, more than 290,000 people visited Costa Rica's national parks. Although tourism is an important industry in Costa Rica, huge numbers of visitors harm some types of plants and frighten small animals. The government responded to the problem by increasing the parks' admission fees in 1994. The fee increase led to a slight decrease in the number of visitors.

To further safeguard the country's environment, the government plans to hire foreign environmental experts and buy more land to place under protection. It has also been actively seeking the cooperation of Costa Ricans to stop hunting species for which the parks are a refuge. Despite these efforts, illegal hunting, mass deforestation, and the dumping of toxic wastes continue to harm Costa Rica's national parks.

The Quetzal

People travel great distances to catch a glimpse of the quetzal, the national bird of Guatemala. Quetzal is also the name of that country's currency. Although the quetzal can be found in almost all of the countries in Central America, it is an endangered species.

Part of the trogon family of birds, the quetzal is known for its long, brightly colored feathers. It measures about 14 inches (36 cm) in length. Both male and female quetzals have greenish-gold feathers, which are blue on the backs. The male has a bright red breast and long, green tail feathers. The male's tail can grow up to 2 feet (61 cm) long. The female quetzal has fewer red feathers on her breast and short tail feathers.

Left: **This male quetzal, with its characteristic long, green tail, camouflages itself well in its surroundings.**

During the mating season, from March to June, the female lays her eggs in an old tree trunk. She and the male take turns sitting on the eggs to keep them warm. After an eighteen-day incubation period, the eggs hatch. The young quetzals stay in the nest for about twenty-one days.

Ancient Belief

The quetzal has long been part of the history of Central America. It was revered by Mayans and Aztecs, who worshiped a god called Quetzalcoatl. These ancient indigenous groups believed the quetzal could not survive in captivity, so the bird came to symbolize absolute freedom. Mayans and Aztecs plucked the bird's feathers and used them for jewelry.

Home of the Quetzal

Costa Rica's cloud forests are home to the quetzal. Cloud forests are formed when the flow of moist air meets mountains and creates a misty atmosphere. The Monteverde Cloud Forest Reserve in Costa Rica is the most popular place to see the quetzal. Scientists estimate that about 1,000 quetzals live in this park. Although thousands of people come to see the colorful bird, many leave disappointed, as quetzals blend easily into their surroundings, often eluding the human eye.

San José: Capital City

New Town at the Mouth of the Hill

San José is the largest city in Costa Rica and home to over one million people. It is perched 3,783 feet (1,153 m) above sea level. Due to the elevation, daily temperatures hover around 72° F (22° C) all year round. Fertile soil and adequate rainfall make the land around the city ideal for agriculture. Its pleasant climate and views of the lush, green mountains make San José a memorable city.

San José was founded in 1737 and was originally called *Villa Nueva de la Boca del Monte*, which literally means "new town at the mouth of the hill." At that time, the city was no more than muddy streets and dilapidated buildings. The name was later changed to San José, after the town's patron saint.

San José started small, with only a handful of residents, but, in the late 1700s, the city began to change when tobacco became a major industry. In the early 1800s, the coffee industry started in San José. The city's soil, fertile with volcanic ash, and the cool climate helped this new crop thrive. Coffee barons, many newly rich from their harvests, built majestic homes in the area. As

Below: **This historic canon in a park overlooks the center of San José.**

Above: **San José bustles with people and cultural activities.**

coffee brought prosperity to San José, the small town soon became a busy city.

In 1823, Costa Rica's capital moved from Cartago to San José. Money from coffee exports financed new buildings around the city. By the early 1900s, San José had become a cosmopolitan city with a strong cultural and financial base. *Josefinos* (ho-say-FEE-nohs), or the people of San José, were greatly influenced by the European way of life, and this influence showed in the buildings they created. The National Theater, built in 1897, is one of San José's most beautiful buildings. Financed by the coffee elite, the theater was embellished with marble and gilded gold.

Today, San José is home to many museums, galleries, and nightclubs. Excellent theater and dance groups, as well as a great variety of international cuisines, can be found all over the city. Many visitors to Costa Rica use San José as a base city and travel around the country from there. Growing tourism and a booming population, however, have had an impact on San José's infrastructure. Air and noise pollution and heavy traffic congestion are growing problems.

Sea Turtles

Of the seven species of sea turtles in the world, six are nearly extinct. Costa Rica is home to five of these species: the green turtle, hawksbill, olive ridley, leatherback, and loggerhead.

In Costa Rica, sea turtles nest on both the Pacific and Caribbean coasts, laying their eggs on the beaches. The protected beaches of Costa Rica's national parks are havens for many sea turtles on the brink of extinction.

Tortuguero Beach is perhaps the best place in the country to view sea turtles in their natural habitat. *Tortuguero*, which means "region of turtles," is located north of the city of Limón on the Caribbean coast. This beach is 22 miles (35 km) long and was established as a national park in 1970. Sea turtles attract an estimated 30,000 visitors to the park every year. Another favorite nesting site is near Tamarindo on the Pacific coast.

Left: **This young turtle is struggling to break out of its shell.**

The sea turtle's mating season lasts from September to November. When the female is ready to lay her eggs, she makes her way to shore. Seclusion is important for sea turtles; bright lights or loud noises send the female straight back into the water. Once on the beach, the female navigates the sand until she finds the perfect spot to dig her nest. She uses her flippers to make a hole, about 2 feet (61 cm) deep, in the sand. There she lays her eggs, usually over one hundred of them, before covering the hole with sand. Then she returns to the water.

Sea turtle eggs incubate for months, and, when they hatch, the young must dig their way out of the sandy nest. Young sea turtles struggle to reach the water, trying to escape dogs, birds, and even humans on the beach. Only about five of every one hundred baby turtles survive the short trip to the sea.

Sea turtles face many threats, and the most dangerous is humans. People hunt sea turtles for their valuable shells, which are used to make jewelry and other luxury items. The turtle's insides make a nutritious soup, a delicacy in many parts of the world. Humans also dig up sea turtle nests and steal the eggs. Turtle eggs are believed to be a strong stimulant and are often served in bars and restaurants throughout the Caribbean and in some parts of Asia.

Semana Santa

Semana Santa, or Holy Week, is celebrated in Costa Rica. Maundy Thursday and Good Friday are national holidays, and offices, shops, and government buildings are closed from Thursday to Sunday. People attend mass regularly, and processions are a common sight, especially toward the end of the week.

Good Friday is a day of mourning for Catholics. In the morning, people attend mass clad in black. At noon, processions through the streets reenact Christ's journey to Calvary, where he was nailed to the cross. No statues are used. Actors portray Jesus and the Roman soldiers who escorted him. The actor who plays Jesus carries a large wooden cross on his back and slowly walks down the street. Large crowds line the roads to watch this dramatic procession.

At the end of the procession, the actor who plays Jesus is "nailed" to the cross. Later, he is taken down from the cross and laid on a special gold platform, which is carried back to the

Below: **Good Friday processions in Costa Rica reenact the Passage of Christ to Calvary. The most beautiful processions take place in big cities, such as Cartago.**

Above: **The actor who plays the role of Jesus hangs from a wooden cross at the end of the Good Friday procession.**

church by a group of men. Little girls, dressed as angels, follow "Jesus" back to the church.

Judas Day

On the Saturday before Easter, people celebrate Judas Day. Judas was one of Jesus' twelve apostles. According to the Bible, Judas betrayed Jesus for money. His betrayal led to Jesus' crucifixion. Judas felt so guilty and ashamed of what he had done that he hanged himself.

On Judas Day, the solemn tone of Good Friday is lifted, and people take part in games and festivities. They play jokes on each other and have lots of fun. Most towns hang an effigy, or dummy, of Judas from a tree.

Easter Sunday

At dawn on Easter Sunday, as people watch and cheer, the effigy of Judas, which is stuffed with fireworks, is burned. The procession of the Resurrection takes place on this day, and towns come alive with joy, as Christians remember the miracle of Christ's return to life.

Volcanoes

"Ring of Fire"

Volcanoes dot the Central American isthmus, the land that connects North and South America. Costa Rica is part of the "Ring of Fire," a volcanic circle that stretches from the western coasts of South, Central, and North America, across the Pacific to Japan and Indonesia, and south to New Zealand. Shifting tectonic plates under the sea floor in this area create this volcanic activity.

Costa Rica is home to seven of Central America's forty-two active volcanoes: Arenal, Barva, Irazú, Miravalles, Poás, Rincón de la Vieja, and Turrialba. These active volcanoes are located within national parks, where visitors can take a close look at them. Costa Rica also has about sixty dormant and extinct volcanoes scattered across the country.

Irazú and Poás

Irazú Volcano, located just outside San José, is perhaps the most visited volcano in the country. At a height of about 11,260 feet (3,432 m), it is the highest volcano in Costa Rica. Irazú Volcano last erupted in March 1963, on the day U.S. president

Below: **Irazú Volcano offers a magnificent view of smoke, clouds, and sky.**

John F. Kennedy made an official visit to Costa Rica. The eruption covered San José and its outlying areas with 5 inches (13 cm) of volcanic ash. Animals and people became ill, and crops were damaged in the Meseta Central. Although the volcanic ash enriched the soil for future crops, it destroyed much of that year's harvest.

Tourists visit Volcán Irazú National Park to climb Irazú Volcano and peer into the green, gaseous lake in the main crater. Irazú has erupted fifteen times in the last 270 years.

Poás Volcano is another active volcano in Costa Rica. It measures 4 miles (6.4 km) wide and has five craters. Poás Volcano has been spouting ash, gas, and sediment into the air for the past thirty years, and it has erupted twenty times in the last 160 years.

Volcanoes' Potential for Good

Although volcanoes can cause mass destruction, they can also benefit entire communities. The Meseta Central has fertile soil, fortified for centuries by volcanic ash, for growing crops. Costa Rica also harnesses the power of Rincón de la Vieja and Miravalles to provide the country with geothermal energy.

Above: **Arenal is an active volcano, rumbling nearly all the time and erupting almost daily. In 1968, a huge eruption killed seventy-eight people. In 1988, an eruption killed one person and badly burned another.**

RELATIONS WITH NORTH AMERICA

Costa Rica has had good relations with the United States and Canada for many years. All three countries are members of the Organization of American States (OAS), which was set up in 1948. This organization aims to strengthen democracy, advance human rights, promote peace and prosperity, expand trade, and deal with poverty and drug problems in the Americas.

The United States assists Costa Rica through the efforts of the Peace Corps, which was established in 1961 by President John F. Kennedy. The corps helps underprivileged people improve their living standards through a variety of programs.

Hundreds of thousands of North Americans visit Costa Rica every year, with the average tourist spending approximately U.S. $1,000 during each trip. A number of Americans have also immigrated to Costa Rica to enjoy its lower cost of living and tropical climate.

Opposite: A white-faced monkey at the Manuel Antonio National Park attracts the attention of curious American tourists.

Below: In May 1997, when U.S. president Bill Clinton (*left*) made an official visit to Costa Rica, he and José María Figueres Olsen (*right*) discussed the importance of protecting the natural environment in both of their countries.

Spreading Peace

The United States and Costa Rica share many common goals. Both countries want to maintain peace in Central America and uphold democracy around the world. In the late 1980s, Costa Rica's president, Oscar Arias Sánchez, led the peace talks that brought about the end of civil war in Nicaragua. The United States, too, played an important role in the peace process.

Nicaragua's troubles began in the 1930s, when the Somoza family came to power in Nicaragua. The family held strict control over the country for the next four decades. Many Nicaraguans were unhappy with the Somozas, and soon, a rebel group called the Sandinistas emerged. By the late 1970s, Costa Rica had become a base for Sandinista troops fighting the Nicaraguan government. In 1979, the Sandinistas took over in Nicaragua, and dictator Anastasio Somoza Debayle fled the country. Sandinista reforms, however, went against Costa Rica's idea of democracy, and Costa Ricans became disillusioned with the Sandinistas.

By 1980, the United States had successfully trained a group called the Contras to fight the Sandinistas. Under pressure from the United States, Costa Rica was forced to let the Contras use the country as a base. In return, U.S. aid flowed into Costa Rica. Peace returned to the region in 1988 when Costa Rican president Arias Sánchez led talks that brought about a ceasefire in

Above: **Anastasio Somoza García ruled Nicaragua as a dictator for twenty years. He was succeeded by his two sons, Luis and Anastasio Somoza Debayle.**

Left: **At a 1998 press conference in Boston, Oscar Arias Sánchez convinced the Central American countries to play a more active role in ending the political upheaval in Panama.**

Left: **Thousands of Costa Ricans line the streets to see U.S. president Bill Clinton's motorcade roll through downtown San José before a summit for leaders of Central American countries. Clinton opened the summit with a message of harmony to expand trade and fight crime in the region.**

Nicaragua. In 1990, the United States and Costa Rica both played crucial roles in creating a safe environment for Nicaragua's democratic elections.

Costa Rica and the United Sates also came to Haiti's aid when, in 1994, Costa Rica strongly supported the United States in a United Nations decision to help end a political crisis in Haiti. Costa Rica then deployed medical personnel to the area.

Aid and Trade

Costa Rica suffered an economic crisis in the 1980s, but with help from the United States, it stabilized its economy. During the crisis, the United States supplied Costa Rica with over U.S. $1.1 billion in aid. In 1994, the aid was reduced to U.S. $3.3 million. Direct financial aid to Costa Rica ended in the mid-1990s.

The United States is Costa Rica's most important trading partner. In 1998, the United States exported U.S. $1.75 billion worth of goods to Costa Rica. That same year, it imported U.S. $1.5 billion in goods from Costa Rica. Currently, over two hundred U.S. companies operate in Costa Rica, with many employing Costa Rican workers. Intel, which manufactures computer chips, recently set up an office in Costa Rica, pumping millions of dollars into the Costa Rican economy.

Free Trade Area of the Americas

The Free Trade Area of the Americas (FTAA), an idea that began in 1994, brings together thirty-four of the Western Hemisphere's thirty-five countries with a mission to establish a free-trade zone from Alaska to Argentina. The FTAA, which includes Costa Rica, Canada, and the United States, represents a market of about 800 million people with a total Gross Domestic Product (GDP) of about U.S. $15 trillion.

The FTAA aims to have free trade by the year 2005, eliminating or reducing the high taxes imposed on imported goods. Both Canada and the United States are interested in expanding their regional presence, although Canada seems the more active supporter of the FTAA. Canada is now in the process of establishing international business networks to further penetrate the Central and South American markets.

In March 1998, the fourth meeting of the Western Hemisphere's trade ministers took place in San José.

Left: **In the late 1990s, U.S. president Clinton (*far right*) and Central American leaders started talks toward creating the world's largest free-trade zone, which would stretch from Alaska to Argentina by the year 2005.**

Left: **McDonald's famous golden arches are a common sight in most of Costa Rica's big cities.**

Representatives discussed the future of the FTAA and elected Costa Rica to chair the Investment Negotiating Group.

Despite criticism of the FTAA, some progress is currently being made toward establishing the largest free trade-zone in the world.

Influences through Trade

Costa Rica is the United States' thirty-ninth biggest export market, so it is inevitable that American products and culture have a great influence on Costa Rican society.

National and satellite television channels show popular American series, and Costa Ricans know more about Hollywood actors than actors from their own country. McDonald's, Burger King, Pizza Hut, and CNN are integral parts of Costa Rican life. Many Costa Ricans prefer the consumerist lifestyle of the United States to their Central American neighbors' non-consumerist lifestyles, which some consider old-fashioned.

Foreign Relations with Canada

Throughout the 1990s, Canada has actively pursued close relations with Costa Rica to strengthen its trading ties and broaden its market to the south.

A Canadian Initiative

In the mid-1990s, Canada established the Canadian Initiative for Industrial Competitiveness (CIIC) in Costa Rica. The CIIC is an agreement between the governments of Canada and Costa Rica that aims to increase product quality, promote female entrepreneurs, and support environmentally friendly business practices in the workplace.

Canada provides technological know-how to Costa Rican companies and receives payment for its services. With Canada's help, Costa Rica hopes to increase its competitiveness in the industrial sector. Medium-sized Costa Rican companies may apply to the CIIC program. Selected companies receive funds and other benefits.

Below: **In 1996, José María Figueres Olsen** (*far right*) **and other Central American leaders met with Canadian prime minister Jean Chrétien** (*second from left*) **in Ottawa, Canada, to discuss trade and other issues.**

Foreign Investment

In early 1998, Costa Rica and Canada established the Foreign Investment Promotion and Protection Agreement (FIPA). The agreement was signed in San José by the Canadian international trade minister, Sergio Marchi, and the Costa Rican minister of external trade, José Salazar. FIPA protects and promotes foreign investment in Canada and Costa Rica, addressing transfers of funds, disputes between the two countries, and the use of property without payment.

Above: **In 1998, Sergio Marchi (*above*) and José Salazar signed the FIPA to promote investment in Canada and Costa Rica.**

Canada and the Central American Common Market

In 1998, Canada signed an agreement with the Central American Common Market, which includes the countries of Costa Rica, El Salvador, Guatemala, Honduras, and Nicaragua. This agreement helps Canada promote free trade and investment in Central America. Ideally, Canada hopes to enjoy free trade privileges throughout the Western Hemisphere.

Peace Corps

The Peace Corps sends American volunteers to developing countries to share their experience and technical know-how in the areas of education, environment, technology, health, business, and agriculture. In thirty-eight years of service, Peace Corp volunteers have helped people in more than 130 countries. Today, there are 6,700 volunteers in the Peace Corps, and the number is expected to reach 10,000 by the year 2003.

How Volunteers Help

Costa Rica is one of the countries receiving aid from the Peace Corps. Volunteers in Costa Rica help young people and families by establishing and administering arts programs, organizing parent-teacher meetings, arranging recreational events, and designing school curricula. They also work with *Patronato Nacional de la Infancia*, or PANI, to improve the lives of children.

Left: **These Peace Corps volunteers are working with a Costa Rican farmer on an agricultural project.**

Drug Trafficking

Drug trafficking is a major problem for the United States. Since it is a large country with a long border and a lucrative market, the United States is a perfect target for drug shipments. Costa Rica, located in the middle of the Central American isthmus, is a central port for drug shipments moving from South America to the United States. Large amounts of cocaine, in particular, are shipped to the United States through Costa Rica.

Costa Rica and the United States have cooperated to develop anti-drug policies and enforcement procedures. The United States Drug Enforcement Agency works closely with Costa Rican police to stop shipments en route to the United States. In 1997, drug enforcement agents seized a record 17,640 pounds (8,002 kilograms) of cocaine and 66 pounds (30 kg) of heroin in Costa Rica. That same year, Clinton met with José María Figueres Olsen and other Central American leaders to sign the Declaration of San José, an initiative to strengthen international cooperation and support democratic institutions. In August, Costa Rican leaders met with the U.S. Attorney General, the Secretary of State, and the National Drug Control Policy Director in Washington, D.C. to discuss drug trafficking and transnational crimes.

Above: **This policeman guards a shipment of cocaine that was seized in a trailer near the Panama border.**

North Americans in Costa Rica

Tourism is big business in Costa Rica. Tourists to this small country number in the hundreds of thousands every year, and over 200,000 are Americans. About 80 percent of all tourists who visit Costa Rica are Americans or Canadians.

After spending just a few weeks exploring the Costa Rican countryside, some tourists decide to stay permanently. Some 35,000 Americans live in Costa Rica today. Most of these expatriates, called *pensionados* (pen-see-oh-NAH-dohs) or *rentistas* (ren-TEE-stahs), are retired people who came to enjoy Costa Rica's natural splendor and quiet. Warm weather, a lower cost of living, and the country's peaceful political climate are other attractive features.

Moving In

Foreigners have great opportunities to buy land at affordable prices in Costa Rica. A person does not have to live permanently in Costa Rica or be a citizen to buy land. Although the process of buying homes is often time-consuming, potential buyers are generally not discouraged.

Below: **This resort at the foot of Arenal Volcano is a popular spa among tourists.**

Many Americans buy property in Costa Rica. The U.S. dollar is stronger than the local currency, so Americans can afford to buy large tracts of land and build nice homes. Some Americans use their Costa Rican home as a getaway and live there for only a few months a year.

Above: **Bird-watchers search for the elusive quetzal.**

Squatter Problem

Since about 1980, some tension has existed between the United States and Costa Rica related to Americans buying land in Costa Rica. Some American landowners have voiced their displeasure with squatters, or homeless people, living on their land while they are away in the United States. The landowners do not receive payment or rent from these squatters.

The U.S. government has also complained about land being taken away from Americans for use by the Costa Rican government. The landowners receive little, if any, compensation for their properties, and payments the government does make, usually arrive late. Costa Rican officials claim that Americans sometimes buy land without the correct documentation.

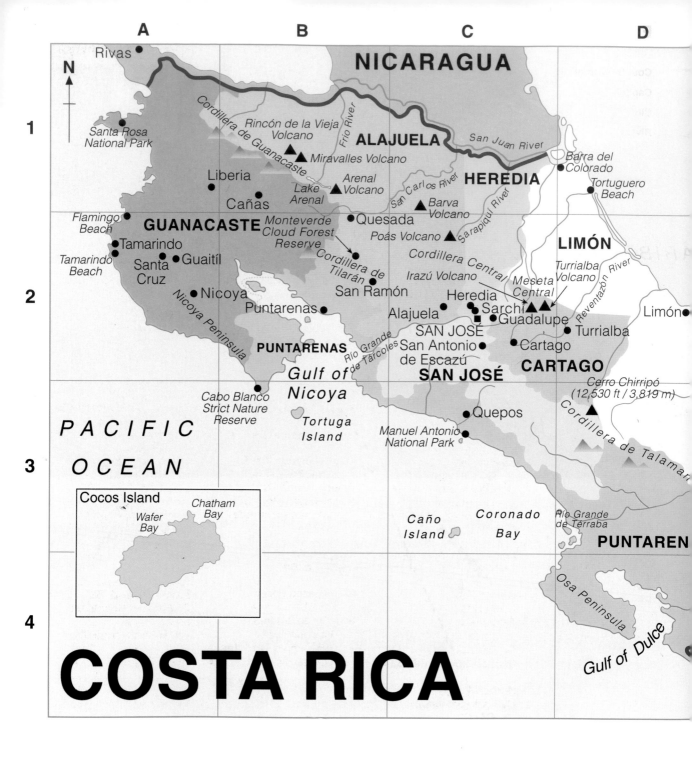

COSTA RICA

NICARAGUA

Rivas

N

Santa Rosa
National Park

Cordillera de Guanacaste

Rincón de la Vieja
Volcano

Miravalles Volcano

Frío River

ALAJUELA

San Juan River

Barra del
Colorado

Tortuguero
Beach

Liberia

Lake
Arenal

Arenal
Volcano

San Carlos River

HEREDIA

Cañas

Barva
Volcano

Sarapiquí River

Flamingo
Beach

GUANACASTE

Quesada

Monteverde
Cloud Forest
Reserve

Poás Volcano

Cordillera Central

LIMÓN

Tamarindo

Cordillera de
Tilarán

Turrialba
Volcano

Reventazón River

Tamarindo
Beach

Santa
Cruz

Guaitíl

Irazú Volcano

Meseta
Central

Nicoya

San Ramón

Heredia

Sarchí

Limón

Puntarenas

Alajuela

Guadalupe

PUNTARENAS

Nicoya Peninsula

Río Grande de Tárcoles

SAN JOSÉ

San Antonio
de Escazú

Turrialba

Cartago

CARTAGO

**Gulf of
Nicoya**

Cabo Blanco
Strict Nature
Reserve

Cerro Chirripó
(12,530 ft / 3,819 m)

Cordillera de Talaman

PACIFIC

Tortuga
Island

Quepos

Manuel Antonio
National Park

OCEAN

Cocos Island

Chatham
Bay

Caño
Island

Coronado
Bay

Río Grande
de Térraba

PUNTAREN

Wafer
Bay

Osa Peninsula

Gulf of Dulce

COSTA RICA

86

E

- Country Border
- Capital
- City
- River

CARIBBEAN
SEA

PANAMA

Above: In 1955, Nils Olaf Wessberg, a Swede, established Cabo Blanco Strict Nature Reserve on the Nicoya Peninsula.

Alajuela (city) C2
Alajuela (province)
    B1–C2
Arenal Volcano B1

Barra del Colorado D1
Barva Volcano C1

Cabo Blanco Strict
    Nature Reserve B3

Cañas B1
Caño Island C3
Caribbean Sea D1–E3
Cartago (city) C2
Cartago (province)
    C2–D2
Cerro Chirripó D3
Chatham Bay A3
Cocos Island A3–A4
Cordillera Central C2
Cordillera de
    Guanacaste A1–B1
Cordillera de
    Talamanca D3
Cordillera de Tilarán B2
Coronado Bay C3

Flamingo Beach A2
Frio River B1

Guadalupe C2
Guaitíl A2
Guanacaste
    (province) A1–B2
Gulf of Dulce D4
Gulf of Nicoya B2–B3

Heredia (city) C2
Heredia (province)
    C1–C2

Irazú Volcano C2

Lake Arenal B1
Liberia A1
Limón (city) D2
Limón (province) D1–D3

Manuel Antonio
    National Park C3
Meseta Central C2

Miravalles Volcano B1
Monteverde Cloud
    Forest Reserve B2

Nicaragua B1–C1
Nicoya A2
Nicoya Peninsula A2–B2

Osa Peninsula D4

Pacific Ocean A1–E4
Panama E3–E4
Poás Volcano C2
Puntarenas (city) B2
Puntarenas (province)
    B2–D4

Quepos C3
Quesada B2

Reventazón River
    C2–D2
Rincón de la Vieja
    Volcano B1
Río Grande de Tárcoles
    B2–C2

Río Grande de
    Térraba D3
Rivas A1

San Antonio de
    Escazú C2
San Carlos River B1–C1
San José (city) C2
San José (province)
    C2–D3
San Juan River B1–C1
San Ramón B2
Santa Cruz A2
Santa Rosa
    National Park A1
Sarapiquí River C1–C2
Sarchí C2

Tamarindo A2
Tamarindo Beach A2
Tortuga Island B3
Tortuguero Beach D1
Turrialba D2
Turrialba Volcano C2

Wafer Bay A3

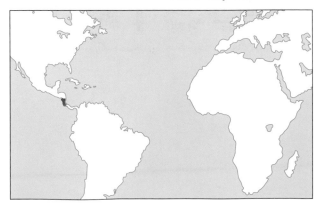

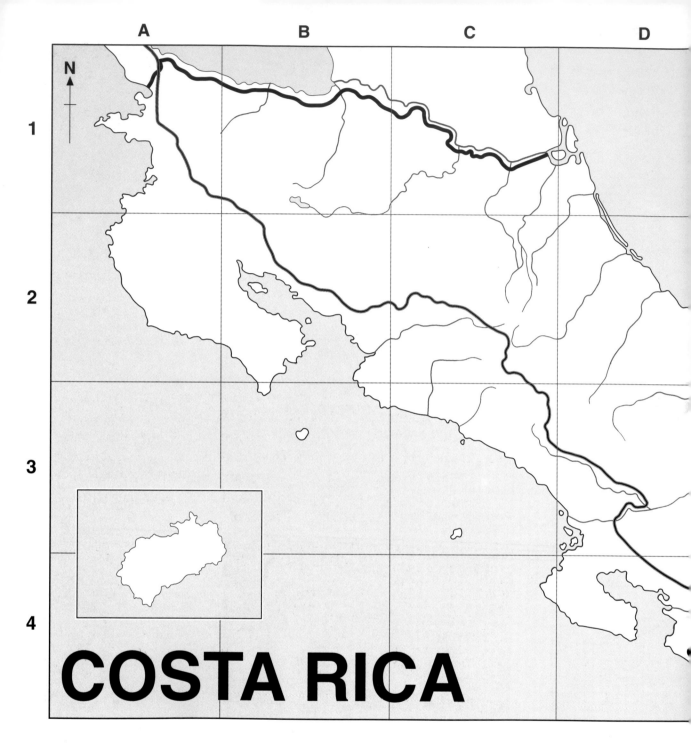

COSTA RICA

How Is Your Geography?

Learning to identify the main geographical areas and points of a country can be challenging. Although it may seem difficult at first to memorize the locations and spellings of major cities or the names of mountain ranges, rivers, deserts, lakes, and other prominent physical features, the end result of this effort can be very rewarding. Places you previously did not know existed will suddenly come to life when referred to in world news, whether in newspapers, television reports, or other books and reference sources. This knowledge will make you feel a bit closer to the rest of the world, with its fascinating variety of cultures and physical geography.

Used in a classroom setting, the instructor can make duplicates of this map using a copy machine. (PLEASE DO NOT WRITE IN THIS BOOK!) Students can then fill in any requested information on their individual map copies. Used one-on-one, the student can also make copies of the map on a copy machine and use them as a study tool. The student can practice identifying place names and geographical features on his or her own.

Above: **Palm trees add to the quiet charm of Tortuga Island.**

Costa Rica at a Glance

Official Name   República de Costa Rica, Republic of Costa Rica

Capital   San José

Official Language   Spanish

Population   3.7 million (July 1999 est.)

Literacy Rate   94.8 percent

Land Area   19,730 square miles (51,101 square km)

Geographical Divisions   Pacific coast, central highlands, Caribbean lowlands

Provinces   Alajuela, Cartago, Guanacaste, Heredia, Limón, Puntarenas, San José

Major Cities   Alajuela, Cartago, Heredia, San José

Highest Point   Cerro Chirripo 12,530 feet (3,819 m)

Major Rivers   Frio River, Reventazón River, Río Grande de Tárcoles, Rio Grande de Térraba, San Juan River

Major Mountains   Cordillera Volcánica and Cordillera de Talamanca

Major Lake   Lake Arenal

Main Religion   Roman Catholicism (95 percent)

Current President   Miguel Angel Rodriguez (elected May 1998)

Famous Leaders   Arias Sánchez, Oscar (1986–1990); Calderón Guardia, Rafael Angel (1940–1944); Figueres, José (1948–1949, 1953–1958, and 1970–1974)

National Anthem   *Noble Patria, Tu Hermosa Bandera* (Noble Homeland, Your Beautiful Flag)

National Flower   Orchid

Important Holidays   Carnival Limón (October), Independence Day (September), La Virgen de Los Angeles (August), Semana Santa (April)

Currency   colón (297.25 = U.S. $1 as of December 1999)

Opposite: **The Church of La Merced stands in the heart of San José.**

Glossary

Spanish Vocabulary

abnegado (ahb-nay-GAH-doh): self-sacrificing.

agua dulce (AH-gwah DOOL-say): a drink made of brown sugar mixed into boiling water.

arroz con pollo (arr-ROHS kohn PO-yoh): a popular Costa Rican dish of chicken, or seafood, and rice.

bocas (BOH-kahs) or *boquitas* (boh-KEE-tahs): small snacks, such as soup, chicken wings, or potato chips.

carretas (kah-RAY-tahs): brightly painted oxcarts that have become symbols of Costa Rica.

casado (cah-SAH-doh): a dish made up of rice, beans, eggs, meat, and vegetables.

ceviche (say-VEE-chay): a boca made of fish marinated in spices and juices.

Consejo de Gobierno (kohn-SAY-ho day goh-bee-AIR-noh): the Council of Government that enforces national laws, sets foreign policies, and has the power to veto bills passed by the legislature.

costumbrismo (koh-stoom-BREES-moh): the use of local settings and characters in Costa Rican literature.

Día de las Culturas (DEE-ah day lahs kool-TOO-rahs): a festival that commemorates Christopher Columbus's arrival in Costa Rica on September 18, 1502.

Día de los Boyeros (DEE-ah day lohs boy-AIR-ohs): an annual festival for oxcart drivers in San Antonio de Escazú.

fincas (FEEN-cuhz): large plots of land on which coffee bushes are grown.

gallo pinto (GUY-yoh PEEN-toh): a breakfast dish of black beans and rice.

huevos de tortuga (HUAY-vohs day tor-TOO-gah): a boca made of turtle eggs.

invierno (een-vee-AIR-noh): winter, or the rainy season, in Costa Rica.

josefinos (ho-say-FEE-nohs): people living in San José.

machismo (mah-CHEES-moh): the attitude that men are superior to women.

marianismo (mah-ree-ahn-EES-moh): the attitude that female behavior should emphasize self-sacrifice.

mestizos (mays-TEE-sohs): people of Spanish and Indian ancestry.

posadas (poh-SAH-dahs): a Costa Rican tradition in which neighbors visit each other's homes at Christmas time, reenacting the journey of Joseph and Mary to Bethlehem.

punto guanacasteco (POON-toh gwon-ah-kass-TAY-koh): a Costa Rican dance that involves a lot of stomping.

sabaneros (sah-bah-NAY-rohs): Costa Rican cowboys.

Semana Santa (say-MAHN-ah SAHN-tah): Holy Week.

Ticos (TEE-kohs): a nickname Costa Ricans use to refer to themselves; also a suffix used to form a diminutive.

tortillas con queso (tor-TEE-ahs kohn KAY-soh): a boca made of tortillas and cheese.

verano (vay-RAH-noh): summer, or the dry season, in Costa Rica.

Virgen de los Angeles (VAIR-hen day lohs AHN-hail-ays): Virgin of the Angels, the patron saint of Costa Rica.

English Vocabulary

assimilated: integrated.

barons: powerful and, usually, wealthy people who control a particular industry in a country.

Central America: the area of North America that connects Mexico with South America and consists of Belize, Costa Rica, El Salvador, Guatemala, Honduras, Nicaragua, and Panama.

deforestation: the large-scale cutting down or destruction of trees.

delicacy: rare, expensive, and tasty food.

dilapidated: in bad condition, often due to neglect or misuse.

diminutive: a word indicating small size or the quality of being familiar, lovable, or pitiable.

dormant: inactive.

European Union (EU): an economic and political organization, formed in 1993 that includes most of the states of Western Europe.

haven: a safe, secure place.

incubation: a period in which birds keep their eggs warm, usually by sitting on them, to promote their development before they hatch.

indelible: permanent.

indigenous peoples: groups of people who originated in the place they presently live, instead of coming from some other country.

isthmus: a narrow piece of land connecting two large areas of land.

Latin America: the countries of Central and South America, Mexico, and the West Indies, where Spanish, Portuguese, or French is spoken.

legacy: an object or idea handed down from the past.

machete: a big knife with a wide blade.

matador: a bullfighter.

New World: the name given by early European explorers to the area that is now North and South America and their surrounding islands.

Nobel Prize: a prestigious award presented to an individual for making an important contribution in one of six fields: physics, chemistry, medicine, literature, economics, or peace.

quetzal: a Central American bird with green and red plumage.

quota: the share or proportion assigned to each member of a body.

resplendent: brilliant.

salsa: a type of dance or music that combines rhythm and blues, jazz, and rock.

squalid: dirty, wretched.

United Provinces of Central America: a union, which lasted from 1823–1840, of the Central American countries of Costa Rica, El Salvador, Guatemala, Honduras, and Nicaragua; also known as the Central American Federation.

worldwide economic crisis of 1929: a period of global economic problems triggered by the U.S. stock market crash in 1929 and lasting until the beginning of World War II.

More Books to Read

Biodiversity. Dorothy Hinshaw Patent (Clarion Books)

The Central Americans. Peoples of North America series. Faren Maree Bachelis (Chelsea House)

Children Save the Rain Forest. Dorothy Hinshaw Patent (Cobblehill)

Costa Rica. Cultures of the World series. Erin Foley (Benchmark Books)

Costa Rica. Enchantment of the World series. Marion Morrison (Children's Press)

Costa Rica. Major World Nations series. Tricia Haynes (Chelsea House)

Costa Rica in Pictures. Visual Geography series. Sandra Sawicki (Lerner)

Discovering the New World: The Voyages of Christopher Columbus. Great Explorers series. Andrew Langley (Chelsea House)

Kids Who Walk on Volcanoes. Paul Otteson (John Muir)

The Monkey Thief. Aileen Kilgore Henderson (Milkweed Editions)

The New Key to Costa Rica. Beatrice Blake (Ulysses Press)

Quetzal: Sacred Bird of the Cloud Forest. Dorothy Hinshaw Patent (William Morrow & Co.)

Videos

Costa Rica. (IVN Entertainment)

Travel the World By Train: Central America. (Pioneer Video)

Wonders of the Deep: Costa Rica/Cocos Island/Galapagos. (Madacy Entertainment)

Web Sites

www.gakkos.com/silent/science/costa/index.htm

www.odci.gov/cia/publications/factbook/cs.html

www.cocori.com/library/crinfo/nutshel.htm

www.costarica.com

Due to the dynamic nature of the Internet, some web sites stay current longer than others. To find additional web sites, use a reliable search engine with one or more of the following keywords to help you locate information on Costa Rica: *Atlantic Railway*, *coffee*, *Franklin Chang Diaz*, *José Figueres*, *Guanacaste*, *quetzal*, *rain forests*, *San José*, and *volcanoes*.

Index